I0828178

FINISHING LINE PRESS
www.finishinglinepress.com

Ask River

poems by

Sara McAulay

Finishing Line Press
Georgetown, Kentucky

Ask River

ISBN 979-8-89990-400-4 First Edition

ACKNOWLEDGMENTS

Thanks to the journals and anthologies where the following poems first appeared, often in somewhat different form:

The Atlanta Review: "Old Agnostic's Praise Song"
Hole in the Head Review: "After you interrogate the empty sky,"
"on doonerak time"
Persimmon Tree: "Forsythia"
Pine Row Press: "Letter to the Child in the Tree"
*Sky Island Journa*l: "Cloudburst," "When the storm broke"
Stone Poetry Journal: "Mud Dog"
Synkroniciti: "chesapeake," "High Wire," "In the beginning,"
"One That Got Away"

Publisher: Leah Huete de Maines
Editor: Christen Kincaid
Cover Art: "Streaks" by John Oughton; https://joughton.wixsite.com/imagenery
Author Photo: Susan Bender
Cover Design: Elizabeth Maines McCleavy

Order online: www.finishinglinepress.com
also available on amazon.com

Author inquiries and mail orders:
Finishing Line Press
PO Box 1626
Georgetown, Kentucky 40324
USA

Contents

High Wire

Hanging by her knees
from the high wire
of impulse
she sees things from
an unfamiliar angle—

wings in Vs
skate cloud to tree-
top across a lake
of glacial blue.

All birds look black
against noon sky—
that high
their birdness blurs
in mid-day glare.

They could be fish.
They could be hands
opening to gesture,
closing into fists.

One by one by one
by one
they strike the sun
and disappear.

Old Agnostic's Praise Song

Why choose me, knowing I don't believe?

Your long arm casting half a heart, setting free this day
in pricks of light and miracles

≈

that I awoke again this morning
that my feet can find the floor
that I can find my feet at all

and when I find them, free of tangled dreamsheet
and the sleeping dog, do you see

≈

how prayerfully I lower them
(though I refuse to pray)
toward worn black leather slippers

≈

how carefully I pour my coffee
how I honor gravity
not a drop allowed to spill

≈

how reverently I line up
my many modern-science pills
and wash them down—

≈

a tart and tingling glass of Thou
Shalt Nots

If I leave my house, stroll out onto the world
will I find another day of random blessings
to not-believe in?

≈

accordionist on the corner
old couple waltzing to Beer Barrel Polka

Tamales Celestiales open before noon
to feed us all

I can't be bribed, you know that. Still

≈

no drive-by shot has killed me yet
bank robbers and bolt lightning wait
until I leave to strike

Do I believe in luck, in accident?
Why not? Still

I don't rule out

≈

long walks by the water, bare toes
in gritty sand, a tide-washed log to sit on

the tennis ball my dog
drops at my feet

Always I believe in evening's long
and glittering arc

≈

brown pelican, blue heron, snowy egret
skyline, bridge and mountains

always and never changing

≈

o blessed circling planet o blessed watchful
sun o blessed late-day shadows

pine and cypress
moon riding shotgun
at my shoulder

After you interrogate the empty sky

ask River as it wraps its tender
jaws around your legs: how does it know

whose bones are whose? Ask these bones
now, as someone, someday, will ask

yours: did you hear the river call? Did your
blood press forward electric

in your legs, your breast, bringing you
here, inevitable as the stream

toward ocean's call, past trees, past shadows,
past wrens and finches going on

about their lives? Now raise your eyes
again. Ask Sun,

ask Earth: in what order
and by what design have these unbroken

hidden circles been the heart
of song? Birth to death, Sun orbits

Earth inside the human heart. Look up:
bellies of lenticulars, curded cumulus,

long lift and sweep of silk-
strand cirrus—vaporous

illusions, tricks of dust mote, light
and air. Ask why we dirt-foot humans turn

our gazes skyward in our search
for god or good or wisdom? Why pray

heaven help us? Why not *river*
help us, mountainside and lowland

see us safely home?

In the beginning

was the lake   no   the rain   and I was alone in it
alone in the clash   of warm and cool   wind and darkness
planets   stars   something in the air   bumping against something
else   sharp elbows   hard shoulders   in the soft disguise of clouds
holding tight the storm   and then the rain
In the beginning was the rain   and I was alone in it
alone with the lake   the river   the stream   water you could drink
In the beginning   hummed the pulse   flowing through mud
and over stones   and I was alone with it
until the planes dropped low   trailing acrid plumes
first the aphids died and the borers   then the fish   the native trout
and bass
hardy catfish   grew warts   grew extra fins   as the frogs died
and the birds that ate the frogs
I have seen a river   tainted by mine tailings   reclaimed by song
by the urgency of many guitars
I have seen fires   parched canyons   torched pines   a boiling river
but I was not alone
In a parking lot   we held each other   a mountain burning mad
through the night
a fire   a fear   unquenched by rain or singing

Cloudburst

thin pasture
threadbare green corduroy
          drought-stricken   dry-grass
tickle in the nose
eased by afternoon downpour—
          rich stink   mud and manure
                    after rain

beyond the hills the river rising

drought or flood
this clay holds stories:
          cipher channels carved and scratched—
patient root and rhizome hold
          arrowheads   hold musket balls
                    hold shards and skulls
                              a treasury of teeth

here and there, paralyzed with rust, a length of chain

red mud ooze
          beside the moody occoquan
                    rain-fed currents lap
and nibble slumping banks
half-hidden fossil sharks and mussels
          carcharhinaformes
                    chesapecten nefrens

myocene to pleistocene—child's summer collected
in a jar

cloudbursts soak us all
rising rivers suck our teeth
                    and bones deep down
to memory
to myth

on doonerak time

        everyone fears something ~ joe the guide

solstice sun
yellow yoyo on a string
        circling
                mount doonerak
                        circling
        the rotting glacier
mango orange in arctic light
        river rapids lined
                with bones

charlie the marine from southern cal
had been in ‘nam
        he was afraid of bears
                        still more afraid
                that joe the guide would
        smell his fear and laugh

i wasn’t afraid
but then the swollen river snared
my ankles, sucked me under, spat me out
        a hundred yards downstream
                tongue gritty with silt
teeth screaming

the calm indifference of it
the *do not give a shitness* of it

fireweed rings a tussock meadow
three little tents on aprons
        of soft moss, lichen,
                    coltsfoot
        a dozen kinds of saxifrage
thawing permafrost below
impersonal, hungry as the river

but we're in the sky up here, far above
the arctic circle, far above
          the treeline
                    glacier runoff sliding
                              down the mountain's face
          like sweat
far above our lives below—
          analog twitch of all we thought
          we knew replaced
                    by the *tick*
                              tick of rotting ice
yellow yoyo winding time on its tether

charlie says he dreams of teeth
what did the river taste
          when it closed its mouth around me?

charlie was the one
who grabbed my shirt that day
          who stood me on my feet

now in yellow solstice sunrise i feel him
listening wide eyed to the growl that's not
a bear

tundra, a word like thunder
          stones tumble in the shallows
                              loons' cries stand
                    the hair up on my arms

outside my tent dawn's arc
sweeps, wind flattens fireweed
          shadows peel free

                    becoming birds
          becoming fears

becoming ice and air.

One That Got Away

down they forgot as up they grew ~ e.e. cummings

There was muscle in the brush, life-blood
in the ink: snake and camel, mouse and whale—
I drew them and they breathed.

On the wall next to my bookcase, home of Bagheera
and Shere Khan, I sketched a storm-lashed ocean,
islands, Tarzan jungles. Curl-tailed blue tigers

flew up from my brushstrokes, chased
by singing fish. *What have you done?* My mother.
Hands on hips, eyes narrowed at the web of lines

and dribbles—bloodless creatures dull as dust,
drained of their magic by her grown-up stare.
Young lady—as she turned back toward the hall—

you'd better get a sponge.

That night I moved my bookcase, hid the smudges
on the wall. I lined up Pal the Flannel Horse, Red
Rabbit, Dingo Dog and others, nameless now,

and *pow!* I shot them—thumb stiff and finger
pointed—shot them dead, then cried, then
brought them squeaking, barking back to prance

again from floor to bed to bureau top to living air, where
        pow!
again I shot them
        pow! !
again
        and brought them back
again
        to roar   and sing
                                        and fly.

Beachcombers

Wake before the stars burn out.

Barefoot, shrugging into shirtsleeves, race down and down the stairs through predawn birdsong. Salt bay breathing to itself, to you.

Breath-stories rise and fall with black-glass waves, skims of pelicans mirrored upside down beneath the moon.

At your back, night's high tide traced by chains of drying foam. Secrets in an ancient alphabet you have just begun to learn:

> *spirula* clamshells
> *certiidae* cockles

enormous heart-shaped teeth, *megalodon* drying at tide's edge.

≈

Like the tide, the scientist is always here before you. White hat and yellow knapsack, always far ahead, always almost out of sight.

A real—a *famous!*—scientist, hands cradling a skull. *National Geo* cover on your father's desk.

In dreams you excavate with your own hands a bear-dog femur from the Eocene—frozen bone-shaped stone, open as a singing throat.

Myocene to Eocene, tide turning.

Knee deep now in cold salt dawnlight, fingers trailing foam-rimmed swells. Stoop from time to time to gather

> *odontocete*
> *mysteceti*

these names of other lives
these songs from other worlds

Mud Dog

Your DNA says *Round 'em up*. Your work: to find
what's fled and bring it home. No sheep in sight
so you make do, herd pugs and beagles at the park.

Out on the bay, scattered ducks offend your sense
of order: strewn puzzle pieces, broken things
your blood is called to mend.

Low tide, windy winter morning. We've had our run—
you've gathered up some terriers, chased a ball.
I've had my hour to breathe-not-think. Today

my mind's a knot that won't let go: her mind untied,
speech that darts like startled birds, pan blazing
on the burner yet again. I'm out of Ativan.

It's three o'clock. Tide channel on our left
a thick dark soup of mud and cast-off tires.
Herons pose on long stick legs, spear beaks poised,

alert for lunch. You're at my side, nose to the wind
then porpoise-plunging downstream, belly deep.
Sandpipers spiral, cast across the sun, dip

to feed again as you keep watch, tail so wet
it barely wags. Your work is done, feathered sheep
returned to shore. Bounding from the channel,

nose streaked with who-knows-what,
you race me to the gate. Ordinary safety, bleak beauty
of a little asphalt parking lot. Red Toyota

soaking up the winter sun. The leash snap clicks.
Let's go! You pull toward home, toward warmth
and food. Keys in my hand. My car a long,
long trek away.

Snail

In the streetlight's glow a trail of brightness slants
across a flagstone path from one damp patch of earth

to another, half hidden by spent daisies
and I imagine all I need for safety is to make myself small

and round, grow armor, grow eye-stalk horns, a single, sticky
foot on which to ripple secret to wet secret under cover of night.

Beneath the sun's accusing stare I'll tuck my soft self small
inside my spiral shield, cling to the cool side

of a stoneware bowl and wait for night to come.
What do I dream of, waiting out the day? Leaves

moist and sweet, a thunderstorm, silver
crisscrossed messages: news of my borrowed kind.

Curled in my spiral world, sheltered from the human
gnash and squeal I've left behind. The hours tick past.

When shadows spread and thicken, when there's no sound
but dogs in the distance, flap and flutter of a plastic bag

tossed by the gritty wind, when passing headlights
probe the night, crown lights winking

red and blue, and pass on by—
this is as safe as it gets.

You can cross now.
You can try.

currents

an octopus
in full billow
an opening
umbrella
shades flounder and crab
those avid bottom feeders

shapeshifter microplastics
soft spokes spread
polystyrene / nitrile flecks then furled
muscle-fluid fingers *bottom-bound*
balloons carve currents / strum shafts
of ocean light *storm-drain sludge*
red-dirt scrape & flood dark kelp
wafting / *burned out* electrophorus eels
belly-up bulbs coil /
/ recoil *aluminum foil*
above decaying reefs

motes of cryptostardust spark *medical waste (generic)*
industrial / agricultural waste (ditto) and tumble
as they always have—
radioactive waste / glittering churn (see above)
entangled now *money made & money lost*
with *duct tape* other currents
fishing line other tides

flat white sun at midday *stretch wrap*
sightless eye
wine bottles milk jugs juicejugs sodacans
dead island floating ghost tentacles
tubes & tires & drinkingstraw nasal probes
streaming filmshrouds billowing *bellyup*
bungie cords fishnet pantyhose
past bonewhite reefs in rust-red currents
polystyrene PVC
all but invisible impaled on broken barnacles

zip ties zippers ziplocks
snagged on shells and skeletons
bubble wrap on gaping cephalopod
knots and strands and ropes and chunks of
beaks
plastic

When the storm broke

we broke for cover. Forgetting what we knew, we crouched
beneath tall trees and sheltered close behind slick slabs of
granite laced with iron ore. Hot blue fingers flicked and
probed. A tree caught fire. We felt the mountain flinch.

When the storm broke
strange creatures left the river, climbed the banks and
walked, awkward on two legs. We saw their tender newness,
felt the amniotic river peeled from their skin by pelting rain.

When the storm broke
our legs were tangled branches, lips laced with bourbon,
hands busy. We were awkward as beginners. Outside,
thunder galloped. Our bedroom jumped and sparked.
Bottle, glasses on the table winked electric blue.

I felt the space
between our heartbeats pulse. We clung to each other, to the
loose rings of our hot, glowing lives. Your face flared, flared
again, lover and stranger, in flash and afterglow. Intake of
bright breath in the dark.

Forsythia

A child, breath fogging morning window, backyard
frozen hard and slick. Jays and ravens skitter, pick
at gritty snow still slumped against the fence. Tall
winter-bare forsythia, brittle-black in February's fist,

hides the seldom-used back gate. *Invasive—*
her mother's word. *They'll put down roots, send up*
new branches, take over if we let them, their energy
a threat. Her father would have understood

their arching thrust. *Let's find Andromeda* he'd say
long past bedtime, eye to his telescope. Her father,
in the ground almost a year. *His soul's been saved*
says Reverend Bill. Her mother wars

with weeds. The garden stands at stiff salute
and faces front. Forsythia resists, leaves clinging
past first frost. It blooms too soon. Its long
wild arms semaphore its secrets past her ears.

That ugly shrub, her mother says. *We'll let it stay*
for now, for privacy. Don't let it spread.
It spread and sprawled all summer, new growth
knifing through, becoming wiry limbs the child

can gather close, weave tight. A room, dim earth-
smelling place to bring the unfledged birds,
the squirrels and chipmunks rescued from the dog—
when rescue failed, to bury them. Her father.

In the ground. His soul saved in a bank called heaven,
though she knows he'd rather be a star.
Breath fogging morning window, the child blinks,
then clears the chilly pane. Yesterday's bone-black branches

touched now by early sun. Thready galaxies of promise.
Tomorrow's yellow bloom.

The creek

wound its weed-choked way past the country store, down through the ravine past our summer cabin. The creek had a name: Dedsqua, a nonsense word. When *we discovered America*, my brother told me, *we named things whatever we wanted.* But one afternoon as I sat on the bank, weaving fern bracelets while my brother and a friend skipped stones, the run-together syllables ripped open, jumped apart:

Dead

Squaw

The skin of the creek cracked and sparkled, twisting in sunlight slanting through clouds. *Who was she? Somebody that died in this creek?* The boys looked at me. *Pocahontas?* said my brother, grinning. His friend shrugged. *Probably a name somebody just thought up. Can't have a creek run through your land and not give it a name.*

≈

Inside the water's skin
she took on shape—
cat's cradle of her ribs
the pale measured scrape
of her spine, cracked skullglobe
grinning through the weeds.

Below the water's flowing flesh
I saw her, bones turning, trapped
in the pool with the leeches,
dead branches, lost land,
lost stories carried downstream
with the liquid syllables
of her name.

Accohannock.
Piscatoway.
Pocomoke.

Can't have a creek run through your land….

where edges meet

if you take up this corner, the neat fold
where sky tucks in beneath horizon
if you take that corner in your hand
and draw it to your heart

if you pluck loose this other corner,
that tangle where in some crumpled
otherness the sky's wide hands splayed
open, split a seam through which

an ocean poured, alive with ghosts
and fish—if you draw this wet selvedge
to your heart as well, and gather
from beneath your feet

the hallway between mountains,
the canyons of the cities, holding,
holding, the chambers and vessels

of all your heart

sleep now

your job is done

chesapeake

hiss and sigh and
hiss   sharp slap   waves smack
beaky kayak cheek
            wrinkled membrane   bounce and
twist   black swells bucking
boom and hiss
            sinew   muscle
hiss and boom

dangle your legs in green sea-tangle
frayed hemp tethers shore to childworld rocking
cheek and naked chest pressed to such freedom.
press your ear against rough planks and listen
past flaked paint and splinters for the song
            jingle and slap   (echo)
                                    ...ngle .nd ...p

four hollow drums it takes to float
one neap tide raft   four steel
shells singing
            jingle and slap   (echo)
                                    ...ngle .nd ...p
slubjous tune for child-sized island's
heave and plummet
dead-fish rot glues plank to plank
            sweet stink
            dying and sustaining
hiss and boom

sit   dangle your legs
see your liquid ankles
swirl beneath the water's skin
            feet wavering
                        alive
a pair of fringe-edged fins

Letter to the Child in the Tree

Keeper of secrets, student of squirrels—
the acorns they stow in your mother's tulip bed
become the eyes of dragons.

Kiddo, no seed you thumb however deep
into the earth will watch you grow, follow you
down steep granite onto the sand.

No limb to hold you now, no teacher versed
in seaweed scrawls to help decipher stars
and messages washing toward your bare feet

from worlds away—how you saw it clear
for just a moment: Earth, a shallow bowl
resting in a deeper bowl, rocked in one cupped hand.

Sara McAulay grew up in northern Virginia and spent summers barefoot in a bathing suit on the shores of the Chesapeake Bay, collecting shells and sharks' teeth, and digging fossils from nearby cliffs. For a while, she thought she might grow up to be a paleoichthyologist like the father of one of her childhood friends. Instead, she's been a novelist, professor of English and creative writing, horse trainer (jumpers and dressage), dog trainer (agility and scent work), and founding editor of *Tattoo Highway*, an online journal of prose, poetry and art.

The recipient of NEA and New Jersey State Arts Council fellowships in fiction, she's most recently turned to poetry and flash, earning Best of the Net nominations. She lives in the San Francisco Bay Area, where she volunteers at a food bank, enjoys theater, music of all kinds, and hiking in the hills with her binoculars and her dog. Two formerly feral cats keep an eye on things at home.

www.ingramcontent.com/pod-product-compliance
Lightning Source LLC
LaVergne TN
LVHW091813110826
845146LV00006B/1224

* 9 7 9 8 8 9 9 9 0 4 0 0 4 *